MENSA®
ULTIMATE
BRAIN
BENDERS

T0064851

⊕ MENSA®
ULTIMATE
BRAIN
BENDERS

100 Puzzles to Improve Your Memory, Concentration, Creativity, Reasoning, and Problem-Solving Skills

DAVID MILLAR

Skyhorse Publishing

Skyhorse Publishing books may be purchased in bulk at special discounts for sales promotion, corporate gifts, fund-raising, or educational purposes. Special editions can also be created to specifications. For details, contact the Special Sales Department, Skyhorse Publishing, 307 West 36th Street, 11th Floor, New York, NY 10018 or info@skyhorsepublishing.com.

Skyhorse® and Skyhorse Publishing® are registered trademarks of Skyhorse Publishing, Inc.®, a Delaware corporation.

Visit our website at www.skyhorsepublishing.com.

10 9 8 7 6 5 4 3 2 1

Library of Congress Cataloging-in-Publication Data is available on file.

Cover design by Brian Peterson

Print ISBN: 978-1-5107-5884-1

Printed in China

CONTENTS

Puzzles 1

Answer Keys 107

    Black Holes.. 108

    Chess Sudoku.. 110

    Cube Logic 110

    In Memoriam 111

    Numcross.. 112

    Rearrangement... 113

    Rows Garden 114

    Story Logic 115

    Symbol Sums.. 116

    Tetra Grid 117

Exercise Your Mind at American Mensa 119

PUZZLES

Rows Garden 1

Using the clues provided, enter a letter into each triangle to fill the garden. Each row contains one or two entries, and each hexagonal flower contains a six-letter word wrapped around the center. It's up to you to determine where to place the starting letter and the direction of the word.

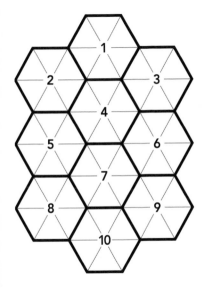

Surname to Scooby or Scrappy

Wrestler Rhodes/Glitzy accessories

Wrongful act/Creative

Dog treat/Chapman on OITNB

"Put a ___ on it!"/Multi-person race

Sara Quin's sis/Dairy producers

Fortune-telling cards/Ready

Everyone's MySpace friend

Flowers

1. With Mary, a drink
2. BBC sci-fi character
3. Greedy
4. Seafaring bandit
5. Oft-tied bit of cloth
6. Instant sports feature
7. Ballet performer
8. Bullseye
9. Arm joints
10. Red fruit

Black Holes 1

Divide the grid into chunks along the guides provided so that each chunk contains one black hole, and so the digits in the chunk sum to the number in the black hole.

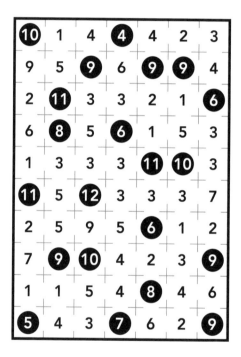

Chess Sudoku 1

Place a digit from 1 to 8 into each empty cell so that each row, column, and 3x3 block contains each digit once, without repetition. The chess knights in the grid display the sum of the digits in the cells which they can attack.

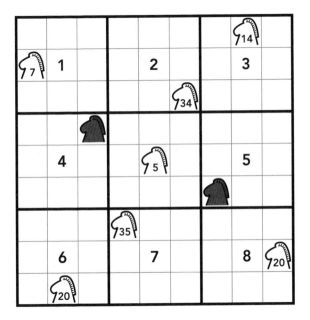

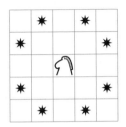

Story Logic 1

'Tis the season for trick-or-treating, and five locals are earning extra cash working at a haunted house. Use the clues to match each person with their haunted house section, the section's theme, and their costume.

		Section					Scene					Costume				
		Section 1	Section 2	Section 3	Section 4	Section 5	Cavern	Cemetery	Crypt	Jail	Sawmill	Goblin	Mummy	Skeleton	Vampire	Zombie
Employee	Jared															
	Kiera																
	Landon																
	Mekala																
	Nupur																
Costume	Goblin																
	Mummy																
	Skeleton																
	Vampire																
	Zombie																
Scene	Cavern																
	Cemetery																
	Crypt																
	Jail																
	Sawmill																

Landon's sawmill scene is somewhere after the scene with the employee in the goblin costume.

Nupur is not dressed as a skeleton or a zombie.

Jared, who works in the jail section, is not dressed in the vampire costume.

Kiera works in section number 2, which is either immediately before or after the cavern scene.

The crypt scene, whose employee is dressed as either a skeleton or a vampire, is before the goblin's scene.

Mekala works in the very first section.

The employee dressed as a mummy works exactly two sections after the jail scene.

The scene with the employee in the zombie costume is directly between the scenes with the vampire and in the cemetery, in some order.

Tetra Grid 1

Drop each of the shapes into the grid in the order provided to spell ten six-letter words. Clues for the words have been provided next to the grid.

Warm-colored metal

Talkative

Cool kitchen appliance

Infrequently

Family of fruits

Coffee-making utility

Utilitarian garment feature

Roadway

Mystery

Worst day of the week

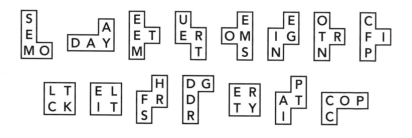

Symbol Sums 1

The sums of five combinations of symbols have been provided. What is the value of each individual symbol?

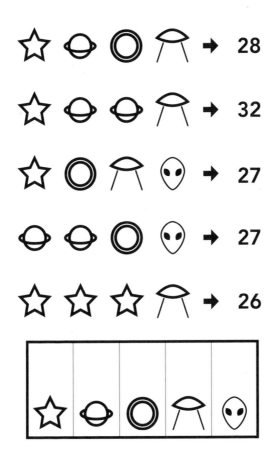

Numcross 1

Use the provided clues to fill the grid with numbers.
No entry may start with a 0.

A	B	C	■	D	E
F			■	G	
■	■	H	I		
J	K			■	■
L		■	M	N	O
P		■	Q		

Across

A.   Emergency phone number in the US.

D.   A down – O down

F.   A perfect square

G.   Another perfect square

H.   J across + O down

J.   D down × 5

L.   O down – 10

M.   Anagram of D down

P.   D across – 1

Q.   A multiple of 4

Down

A.   Half of K down

B.   Square root of F across

C.   2 ^ B down

D.   Anagram of M across

E.   A palindrome

I.   Number whose digits sum to B down

J.   Consecutive digits in ascending order

K.   Part of the name of Tom DeLonge's band

N.   2 × O down

O.   Teaspoons in 1 cup

Black Holes 2

Divide the grid into chunks along the guides
provided so that each chunk contains one black
hole, and so the digits in the chunk sum to the
number in the black hole.

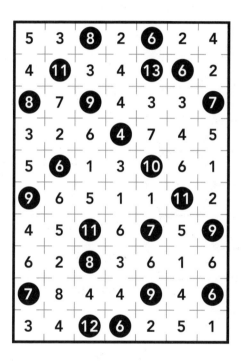

Rows Garden 2

Using the clues provided, enter a letter into each triangle to fill the garden. Each row contains one or two entries, and each hexagonal flower contains a six-letter word wrapped around the center. It's up to you to determine where to place the starting letter and the direction of the word.

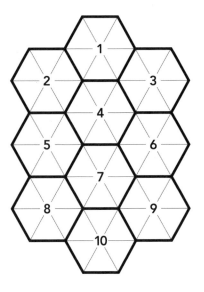

Plead

Dishonest person/Well-suited

Actor Welles/Make a cut

E.g. Superman/Striped animal

News magazine/Clay creature

Chef Lalli Music/Cut back

Ripped/Mistake

Snatch

Flowers

1. Span
2. Naval worker
3. Melatonin gland
4. Wonderful clock button
5. Loner

6. Small glass toy
7. Frozen dessert
8. Dangling horse lure
9. Reflective surface
10. Classic web ad format

Rearrangement 1–2

Rearrange the letters in the phrase "OFFICERS' FLEET" to spell a necessity for keeping caffeinated while on duty.

Rearrange the letters in the phrase "NO BANDIT BARMAN" to spell a crime-fighting duo.

Cube Logic 1

Which of the four foldable patterns can be folded to make the cube displayed?

A

B

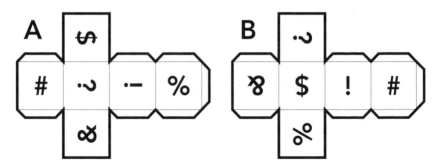

C

D

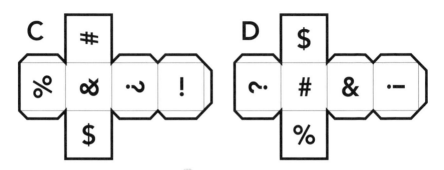

In Memoriam 1A

Memorize the names shown in the list below. When you're ready, turn the page and put your memory to the test.

Aubrey

Becky

Clara

Diedre

Eleanor

Felicia

Grant

Harish

Isabella

Jaspal

Kayla

Luis

Mason

In Memoriam 1B

Moving up, down, left, and right, make a path from
Start to Finish. You may only pass through squares
containing a name from the list on the previous page.

S	Harish	Kelly	Eleanor	Adria
Becky	Greta	Felicia	Aubrey	Grant
Luis	Diedre	Isabella	Louis	Mason
Irene	Kate	Jaspal	Ellen	Kayla
Claire	Didi	Clara	Joss	F

Tetra Grid 2

Drop each of the shapes into the grid in the order provided to spell ten six-letter words. Clues for the words have been provided next to the grid.

One of the Muppets

Savory fruit

Crunchy pad Thai topping

Building material

Take on

Party in Spain

Red suit

An ace in blackjack, often

Smart

NBC/ABC medical comedy

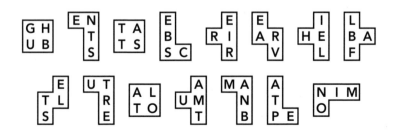

Story Logic 2

Trista's happy hour painting classes are getting scheduled for an upcoming week. Use the clues to match the night with the venue and the painting that will be taught in the class.

		Venue				Painting			
		Georgie's	The Brewery	The Tin Panther	Tres Amigas	Mountains	Sugar Skull	Sunset	Winter Scene
Evening	Sunday								
	Monday								
	Tuesday								
	Wednesday								
Painting	Mountains								
	Sugar Skull								
	Sunset								
	Winter Scene								

The class where a sunset will be painted is after the class at Tres Amigas.

The class at The Brewery is not the first or last class of this set of classes.

The painting of mountains, which will not take place at The Tin Panther, will be on Tuesday evening.

The painting of the wintery scene will either be at Georgie's or The Brewery.

The class at Georgie's will be before the class at The Brewery.

The class for the painting of the sugar skull will not take place at Tres Amigas.

The class teaching the wintery scene painting is set to take place before the class at The Tin Panther.

The painting of the sugar skull is not scheduled for Monday.

Black Holes 3

Divide the grid into chunks along the guides
provided so that each chunk contains one black
hole, and so the digits in the chunk sum to the
number in the black hole.

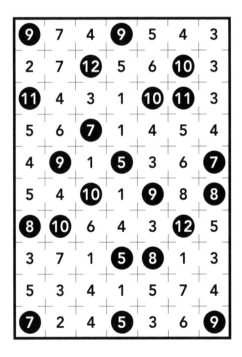

Rows Garden 3

Using the clues provided, enter a letter into each triangle to fill the garden. Each row contains one or two entries, and each hexagonal flower contains a six-letter word wrapped around the center. It's up to you to determine where to place the starting letter and the direction of the word.

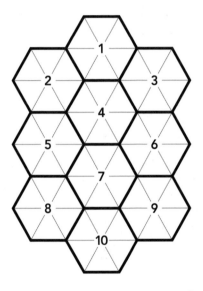

Grappler Anderson

Onlookers/Lack of difficulty

Genie location/Places to live

Antlered beast/First and last?

Farm structure/Garlic units

Hunk of metal/Industrial band

Ellen Pompeo role/E.g. Batman

Competed in a marathon

Flowers

1. Informed of danger
2. Uproar
3. Seed often used in food
4. Often-smart objects
5. Iconic robot vac brand

6. Finds at fault
7. Fastener
8. Spicy root
9. Repeated
10. Bird in a coal mine

Cube Logic 2

Which of the four foldable patterns can be folded to make the cube displayed?

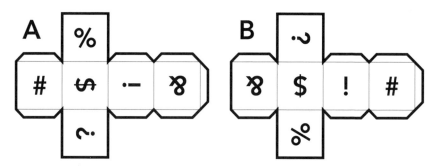

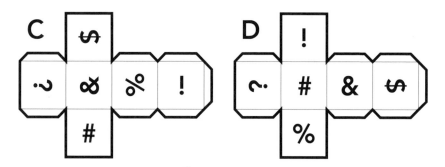

Numcross 2

Use the provided clues to fill the grid with numbers.
No entry may start with a 0.

A	B		C	D	E
F			G		
H		I			
		J		K	L
M	N			O	
P				Q	

Across

A.   A perfect square

C.   G across – P across

F.   A across + 3

G.   L down + 3

H.   K down × F across

J.   Contains every even digit except 0

M.   A multiple of 7

O.   Another perfect square

P.   F across + O across

Q.   Another perfect square

Down

A.   E down + A across

B.   7 × E down

C.   Consecutive digits in ascending order

D.   A prime factor of E down

E.   Balloons in Nena song

I.   M across × 10

K.   One-third of the sum of M across and P across

L.   A palindrome

M.   O across – 10

N.   Q across + 4

Rearrangement 3–4

Rearrange the letters in the phrase "A CORRIDOR'S SIGNAL" to spell a location where you might find a traffic signal.

Rearrange the letters in the phrase "TRENDY HILARITY" to spell a location on a football field where a viral video of a goofy team mascot might be taken.

Symbol Sums 2

The sums of five combinations of symbols have been provided. What is the value of each individual symbol?

☆ ♄ ◎ ⌂ → 57

☆ ☆ ◎ ⌂ → 75

♄ ◎ ⌂ ⌂ → 40

◎ ◎ ⌂ 👽 → 43

☆ ☆ ◎ 👽 → 68

☆	♄	◎	⌂	👽

Tetra Grid 3

Drop each of the shapes into the grid in the order provided to spell ten six-letter words. Clues for the words have been provided next to the grid.

Natural water source

Bolt or screw partner

Random knowledge

Potential movie edible

Plant baby

Earlyish meal

Awfully chilly

Dee Dee's brother with a lab

German neighbor

Like some old film

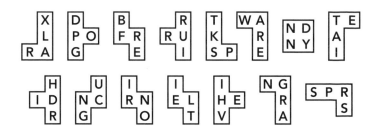

Black Holes 4

Divide the grid into chunks along the guides provided so that each chunk contains one black hole, and so the digits in the chunk sum to the number in the black hole.

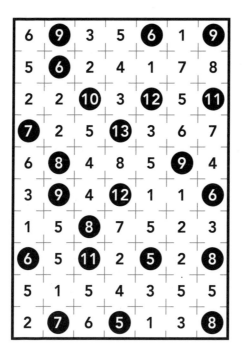

Chess Sudoku 2

Place a digit from 1 to 8 into each empty cell so that each row, column, and 3x3 block contains each digit once, without repetition. The chess knights in the grid display the sum of the digits in the cells which they can attack.

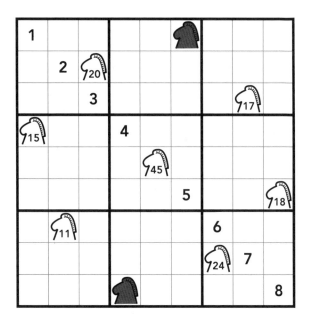

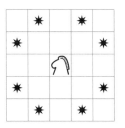

Numcross 3

Use the provided clues to fill the grid with numbers.
No entry may start with a 0.

A	B	C		D	E
F				G	
		H	I		
J	K				
L			M	N	O
P			Q		

Across

A.   A palindrome
D.   A perfect square
F.   One-third of H across
G.   Another perfect square
H.   A down in binary
J.   F across + I down
L.   B down + N down
M.   2 × F across
P.   One-third of A across
Q.   An anagram of D down

Down

A.   B down – 3
B.   Another perfect square
C.   An anagram of I down
D.   A multiple of O down
E.   Comedy Central series Reno ___
I.   Digits that sum to A down
J.   A down × 11
K.   Consecutive digits in ascending order
N.   D down / B down
O.   A&E series The First ____

Rows Garden 4

Using the clues provided, enter a letter into each triangle to fill the garden. Each row contains one or two entries, and each hexagonal flower contains a six-letter word wrapped around the center. It's up to you to determine where to place the starting letter and the direction of the word.

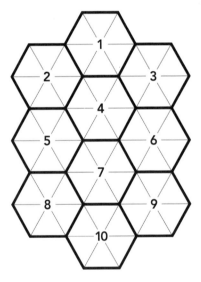

Dedicated creation

Trolley/Criminally smooth

Outbuilding/Push away

Local area or witch/wizard skills

Fad diet/Celestial bodies

Rifle type/Perform like Jay-Z

TV or internet medium/Air out

Former soldier

Flowers

1. Some photo subjects
2. Valentine's Day shapes
3. Preserve in brine
4. Pleasantly unreal
5. Paper for a speeder

6. Cuban exports
7. Share like a meme
8. Woodland dwellings
9. Mom or dad
10. Fuzzy fabric

In Memoriam 2A

Memorize the names shown in the list below. When you're ready, turn the page and put your memory to the test.

Fred

George

Harry

Joey

John

Monica

Paul

Phoebe

Ringo

In Memoriam 2B

Moving up, down, left, and right, make a path from
Start to Finish. You may only pass through squares
containing a name from the list on the previous page.

S	George	Joey	John	Ginny
Rachel	Paul	Ron	Ross	Monica
John	Ringo	Harry	Rachel	Joey
Ross	Chandler	Fred	Ginny	George
Ron	Chandler	Monica	Phoebe	F

Symbol Sums 3

The sums of five combinations of symbols have been
provided. What is the value of each individual symbol?

☆ 🪐 ◎ ⏜ → 21

☆ ◎ ⏜ ⏜ → 24

☆ 🪐 🪐 👽 → 23

🪐 ◎ ◎ 👽 → 28

🪐 🪐 ⏜ 👽 → 29

Cube Logic 3

Which of the four foldable patterns can be folded to make the cube displayed?

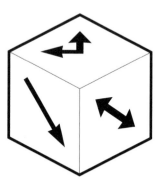

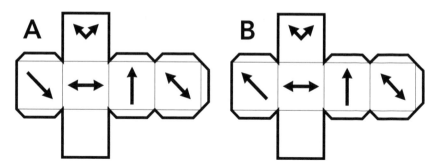

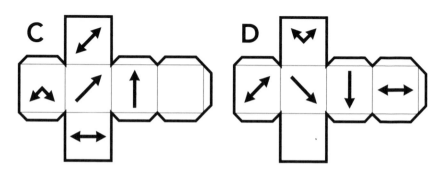

Rearrangement 5–6

Rearrange the letters in the phrase "LOCAL RESTORERS" to spell some attractions that likely require on-site mechanics.

Rearrange the letters in the phrase "ANNEXED ASPHALT" to spell a part of the United States where historic Route 66 once ran.

Black Holes 5

Divide the grid into chunks along the guides
provided so that each chunk contains one black
hole, and so the digits in the chunk sum to the
number in the black hole.

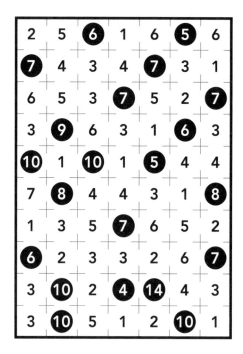

Tetra Grid 4

Drop each of the shapes into the grid in the order provided to spell ten six-letter words. Clues for the words have been provided next to the grid.

Item found above sinks

A bean variety

Flat and clear

Symmetrical shape

Empty

Dairy product

Straightforward

Laminated dough pastry

Do some sightseeing

Post office wares

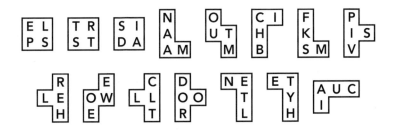

Numcross 4

Use the provided clues to fill the grid with numbers.
No entry may start with a 0.

A	B		C	D	E
F			G		
H		I			
		J		K	L
M	N			O	
P				Q	

Across

A.   One-third of F across
C.   A perfect square
F.   J across / C across
G.   Consecutive digits in ascending order
H.   An anagram of C down
J.   A palindrome
M.   8 × M down
O.   2 × F across
P.   Another palindrome
Q.   Another perfect square

Down

A.   Another perfect square
B.   Digits that sum to N down
C.   2 × P across
D.   Another perfect square
E.   No Doubt single
I.   Consecutive digits in ascending order
K.   L down – 3
L.   P across – M across
M.   A perfect cube
N.   Square root of C across

Symbol Sums 4

The sums of five combinations of symbols have been provided. What is the value of each individual symbol?

☆ 🪐 ◎ 🛸 → 40

☆ ☆ ◎ ◎ → 48

🛸 🪐 🪐 🪐 → 40

🪐 ◎ ◎ 👽 → 52

🪐 🪐 🛸 👽 → 52

☆	🪐	◎	🛸	👽

Rows Garden 5

Using the clues provided, enter a letter into each triangle to fill the garden. Each row contains one or two entries, and each hexagonal flower contains a six-letter word wrapped around the center. It's up to you to determine where to place the starting letter and the direction of the word.

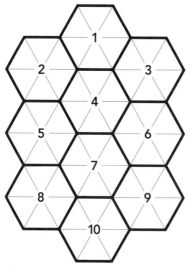

Mighty Mighty Bosstones' genre

Cause harm/Unusual

Center/War machines

Having enthusiasm/"High" shoes

Shaker contents/Strain

Famous twins/E.g. Coke, Pepsi

Baby cow/Partner to "Lost"

Frozen liquid

Flowers

1. Minor adjustments
2. Fried dough treat
3. Bar products
4. Made/kept warm
5. Mouth liquids

6. Arm covering
7. Engine or pump part
8. Folks from nearby
9. Money in London
10. Workplace

Cube Logic 4

Which of the four foldable patterns can be folded to
make the cube displayed?

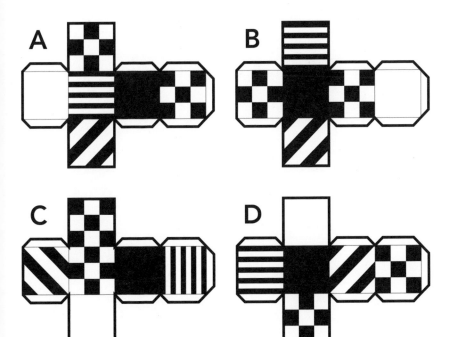

Chess Sudoku 3

Place a digit from 1 to 8 into each empty cell so that each row, column, and 3x3 block contains each digit once, without repetition. The chess knights in the grid display the sum of the digits in the cells which they can attack.

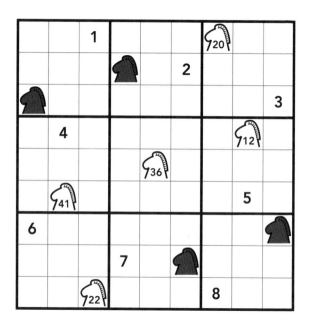

Rearrangement 7–8

Rearrange the letters in the phrase "DARN EAR AGAIN" to spell the name of a pop singer whose concerts might leave your ears ringing.

Rearrange the letters in the phrase "EASE OUT KITCHEN" to spell an option for dinner when you don't want to cook.

Tetra Grid 5

Drop each of the shapes into the grid in the order provided to spell ten six-letter words. Clues for the words have been provided next to the grid.

Colorful autumn sight

Oft-butterflied protein

E.g. Ronald, for McDonalds

Motivated

Adult beverage

Permanent decoration

Grown

Merchant

A connector of places

Rocky road covering

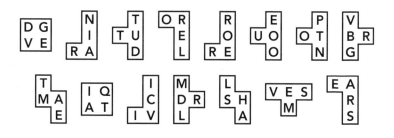

Numcross 5

Use the provided clues to fill the grid with numbers.
No entry may start with a 0.

A	B	C		D	E
F				G	
		H	I		
J	K				
L			M	N	O
P			Q		

Across

A. 5 × F across

D. O down + 7

F. An anagram of K down

G. D across + 6

H. Contains one of every even digit except 0

J. Year US was founded

L. Sum of the digits in J across

M. Digits that sum to P across

P. A perfect square

Q. A palindrome

Down

A. Another perfect square

B. Another perfect square

C. (2 × H across) – 1

D. Consecutive digits in ascending order

E. Classic "page not found" error code

I. Q across × 11

J. Another perfect square

K. One-fourth of H across

N. A down + 7

O. L across + P across

Cube Logic 5

Which of the four foldable patterns can be folded to make the cube displayed?

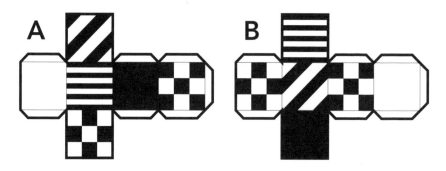

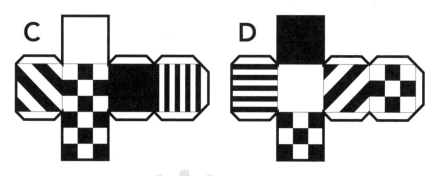

Black Holes 6

Divide the grid into chunks along the guides provided so that each chunk contains one black hole, and so the digits in the chunk sum to the number in the black hole.

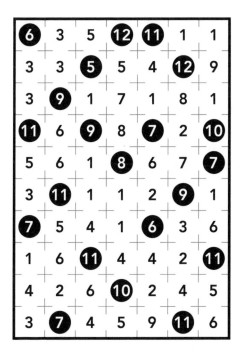

Story Logic 3

A hiking trail at the park is being created. Five new bridges are being added, each at various places along the trail and of different lengths. Use the clues to match the bridge specs with the notable people to which each bridge is dedicated.

		Mile Marker					Bridge Length				
		2.5 miles	2.7 miles	8.1 miles	8.3 miles	9.0 miles	20 feet	32 feet	40 feet	48 feet	60 feet
Dedication	David Biedny										
	Guy Fieri										
	Becky Lynch										
	Leah Remini										
	Adam Savage										
Bridge Length	20 feet										
	32 feet										
	40 feet										
	48 feet										
	60 feet										

The bridge dedicated to David Biedny is the last bridge on the trail.

The longest and shortest bridges are within one mile of each other.

The bridge dedicated to Adam Savage is more than one mile further along the trail than the 60-foot bridge.

The length of the bridge dedicated to Guy Fieri is exactly twice the length of the one dedicated to Leah Remini.

The 32-foot bridge is located at mile marker 8.3.

The bridge dedicated to Leah Remini is not the first bridge along the trail.

Numcross 6

Use the provided clues to fill the grid with numbers.
No entry may start with a 0.

A	B		C	D	E
F			G		
H		I			
		J		K	L
M	N			O	
P				Q	

Across

A. D down + 1

C. A perfect square

F. M down – 4

G. E down × Q across

H. An anagram of I down

J. B down × F across

M. Half of L down

O. N down – 3

P. Consecutive digits in ascending order

Q. 4 × D down

Down

A. Consecutive digits in ascending order

B. F across × 4

C. Start to many toll-free phone numbers

D. 2 × E down

E. Sum of digits in L down

I. Stephen King hotel room thriller

K. B down + G across

L. 5 × B down

M. Another perfect square

N. A perfect cube

Rearrangement 9–10

Rearrange the letters in the phrase "ENCHANT BIGWIG" to spell something that will take place if a TV executive greenlights a great new series.

Rearrange the letters in the phrase "EXACT MONIES" to spell a scenario where precision is very important.

Symbol Sums 5

The sums of five combinations of symbols have been
provided. What is the value of each individual symbol?

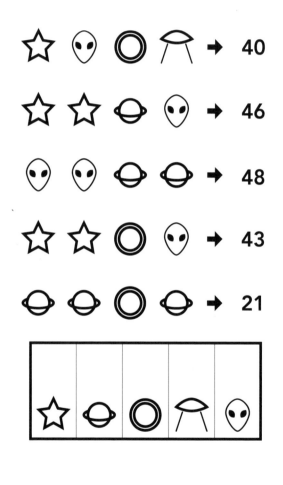

Tetra Grid 6

Drop each of the shapes into the grid in the order provided to spell ten six-letter words. Clues for the words have been provided next to the grid.

Mistake remover

Visit again

Tony organism

A Pacific coast state

Famed chain of "Houses"

Metric units of distance

Bring back

Significant timespan

Waxy light source

Heartbreaking

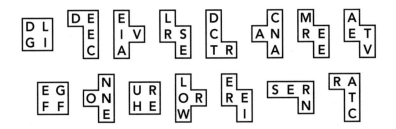

Black Holes 7

Divide the grid into chunks along the guides provided so that each chunk contains one black hole, and so the digits in the chunk sum to the number in the black hole.

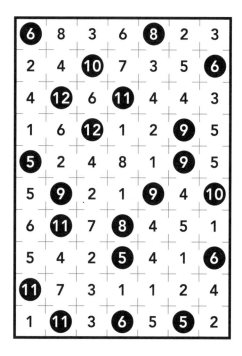

Numcross 7

Use the provided clues to fill the grid with numbers.
No entry may start with a 0.

A	B			C	D
E			F		
	G	H			
		I		J	
K	L			M	N
O				P	

Across

A. A down – 1

C. Sum of the digits in E and F across

E. C across + C down

F. A across × 3

G. O across × C across

I. M across + 10

K. C across × K down

M. L down + E across

O. C down in reverse

P. N down + 30

Down

A. 2 × O across

B. C across × C down

C. C across + 1

D. C across + 2

F. C across × 10

H. 3 × I across

J. L down × 7

K. 4 × D down

L. P across – 8

N. A perfect square

Cube Logic 6

Which of the four foldable patterns can be folded to
make the cube displayed?

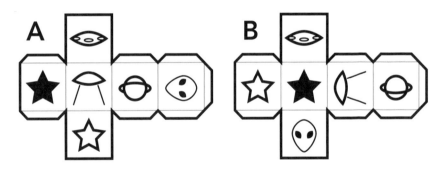

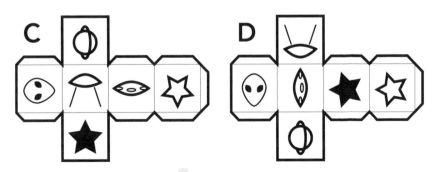

Rearrangement 11–12

Rearrange the letters in the phrase "IT'S ADORATION" to spell a way to hear your favorite band's music.

Rearrange the letters in the phrase "CLEAN GILLS" to spell what you need in order to post fishing trip photos online.

Symbol Sums 6

The sums of five combinations of symbols have been provided. What is the value of each individual symbol?

🪐 🪐 ◎ 🛸 ➡ **37**

⭐ 🛸 🪐 👽 ➡ **51**

👽 👽 ⭐ 🪐 ➡ **52**

⭐ ⭐ 🪐 🪐 ➡ **68**

🪐 🪐 ◎ 🪐 ➡ **42**

⭐	🪐	◎	🛸	👽

Tetra Grid 7

Drop each of the shapes into the grid in the order provided to spell ten six-letter words. Clues for the words have been provided next to the grid.

Popular type of drink

Close

Seasoned

A phase of matter

Conclude prematurely

Dire

Wood-based cooker

Iconic yellow Pixar character

Hair stylist

Like some inbox contents

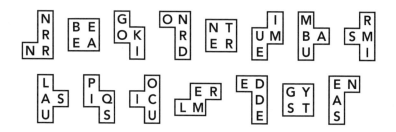

Rows Garden 6

Using the clues provided, enter a letter into each triangle to fill the garden. Each row contains one or two entries, and each hexagonal flower contains a six-letter word wrapped around the center. It's up to you to determine where to place the starting letter and the direction of the word.

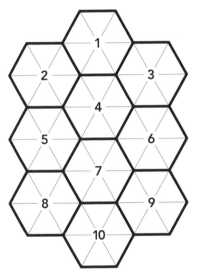

Term of endearment

Hot/Flying toy

Try again/Competitor

Apple part/Garden statue

Edit letter space/Common liquid

Cyclist activity/____ Lanka

Smoothie verb/Amazon device

Make a mistake

Flowers

1. Like some hearty soups
2. 8-legged creature
3. Orate
4. Citrus fruit
5. E.g. Ozzy, Dave Grohl

6. Far away
7. Outdoor partial cover
8. Dry pet food
9. Performing groups
10. Cook down some fat

Black Holes 8

Divide the grid into chunks along the guides
provided so that each chunk contains one black
hole, and so the digits in the chunk sum to the
number in the black hole.

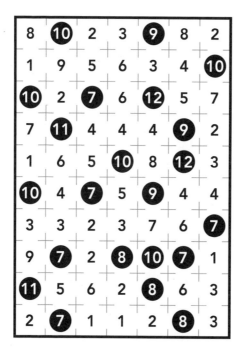

Story Logic 4

This year the local vegan cheezemonger society had its first annual vegan cheeze competition, and the results are in! Use the clues to match the recipe to its author and where their cheeze placed in the standings.

		Award					Cheeze Recipe				
		First Place	Second Place	Third Place	Fourth Place	Fifth Place	Carrot Cheddar	Cauliflower Queso	Nooch-Oh Sauce	Smoked Almond	Walnut Gouda
Cheezemonger	Amy										
	Breighdynn										
	Carol										
	Dirk										
	Eileen										
Cheeze Recipe	Carrot Cheddar										
	Cauliflower Queso										
	Nooch-Oh Sauce										
	Smoked Almond										
	Walnut Gouda										

Neither Carol nor Eileen made Cheezy Cauliflower Queso Dip.

Dirk's recipe placed in the bottom three.

Dirk's cheeze did better than both the Smoked Almond Cheeze Ball and the Cheezy Cauliflower Queso Dip.

The Wild Garlic Walnut Gouda Spread ranked higher than Eileen's recipe, which ranked higher than the recipe for the Smoked Almond Cheeze Ball.

Breighdynn's recipe placed somewhere in the top three.

The Carrot Cheddar Chunks were ranked higher than the recipe presented by Dirk.

Amy did not make the Carrot Cheddar Chunks.

The "Nooch-oh" Cheeze Sauce (featuring "nooch," the nickname of nutritional yeast) placed immediately between Carol's recipe and the recipe for the Carrot Cheddar Chunks in the standings.

Eileen, who did not make the Nooch-oh Cheeze Sauce, ranked either right ahead or behind Breighdynn's recipe in the standings.

Rearrangement 13–14

Rearrange the letters in the phrase "PATINA SCORN" to spell an item that requires a good coat of seasoning before use.

Rearrange the letters in the phrase "TRACTOR IMMUNE" to spell what you might ride to work if you switched from farming to a city job.

Cube Logic 7

Which of the four foldable patterns can be folded to make the cube displayed?

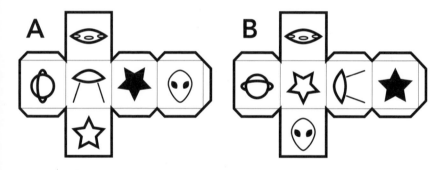

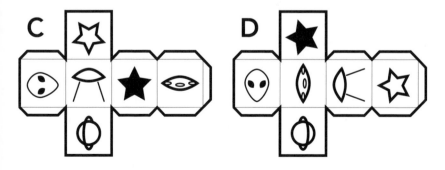

Tetra Grid 8

Drop each of the shapes into the grid in the order provided to spell ten six-letter words. Clues for the words have been provided next to the grid.

NASCAR competitor

Northerner

Woman dating young men

Frying noise

Sharpie product

Part of the US Congress

Sneak attack

Photographer's tool

Group of five letters

Doctrine

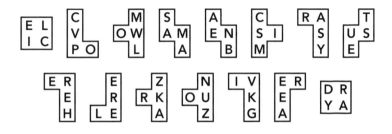

Symbol Sums 7

The sums of five combinations of symbols have been provided. What is the value of each individual symbol?

🪐 👽 🛸 ⭐ → **41**

⭐ 🛸 ◎ 👽 → **30**

⭐ ◎ ◎ 🪐 → **33**

👽 👽 👽 🪐 → **21**

🪐 🪐 ◎ ◎ → **38**

⭐	🪐	◎	🛸	👽

Black Holes 9

Divide the grid into chunks along the guides
provided so that each chunk contains one black
hole, and so the digits in the chunk sum to the
number in the black hole.

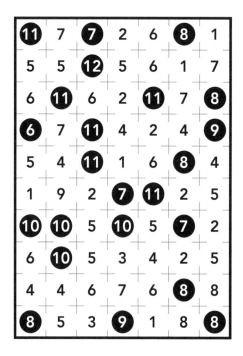

In Memoriam 3A

Memorize the numbers shown in the list below.
When you're ready, turn the page and put your
memory to the test.

Three

Six

Eight

Thirteen

Sixteen

Eighteen

Twenty-two

Twenty-four

Twenty-six

Twenty-eight

Thirty

In Memoriam 3B

Moving up, down, left, and right, make a path from
Start to Finish. You may only pass through squares
containing a number from the list on the previous page.

S	18	16	26	13
3	32	11	22	2
24	21	25	20	6
13	28	8	5	18
10	38	6	30	F

Numcross 8

Use the provided clues to fill the grid with numbers.
No entry may start with a 0.

Across

A.   C across – B down

C.   I down – J down

E.   A down × 3

G.   A across + 5

H.   J across – (13 × L across)

J.   D down × (B down + L across)

L.   Sum of the digits in O down

M.   A across × 6

P.   B down × 2

Q.   O down + L across

Down

A.   N down in reverse

B.   L across + 1

C.   D down + K down

D.   Unique digits that sum to 17, in ascending order

F.   Consecutive digits in descending order

I.   N down × P across

J.   O down × 8

K.   I down + 8

N.   A perfect cube

O.   Another perfect cube

Chess Sudoku 4

Place a digit from 1 to 8 into each empty cell so that each row, column, and 3x3 block contains each digit once, without repetition. The chess knights in the grid display the sum of the digits in the cells which they can attack.

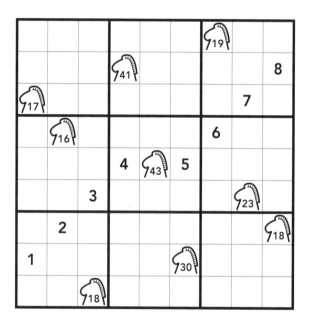

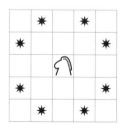

Symbol Sums 8

The sums of five combinations of symbols have been
provided. What is the value of each individual symbol?

🪐 ☆ 🛸 ◎ → 61

◎ 🛸 👽 ☆ → 64

◎ 👽 👽 🪐 → 45

☆ ☆ ☆ 🪐 → 26

🪐 🪐 👽 👽 → 38

☆	🪐	◎	🛸	👽

Rearrangement 15–16

Rearrange the letters in the phrase "LATCHES SETUP" to spell a vehicle that likely has a lot of intricate parts.

Rearrange the letters in the phrase "DEFTEST HEIST" to spell what a robber might encounter if they mistook a linen closet for a bank vault.

Rows Garden 7

Using the clues provided, enter a letter into each triangle to fill the garden. Each row contains one or two entries, and each hexagonal flower contains a six-letter word wrapped around the center. It's up to you to determine where to place the starting letter and the direction of the word.

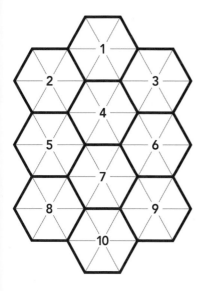

Food container

Like Randy Savage/College tests

Benefit/Desert refuge

Dance or sauce/Zelda protagonist

Artist Salvador/Brave

Nut used in pies/Dedicated

Logician Turing/Smooth move

"Want Ad" acronym

Flowers

1. Chips and cheese
2. Vacation vehicle, often
3. Inactive state
4. Fuzzy Australian "bears"
5. North Texas city

6. Pungent
7. Reptile
8. Royal home or mansion
9. Split apart
10. Not winning

Cube Logic 8

Which two of the six foldable patterns can be folded
to make the same cube?

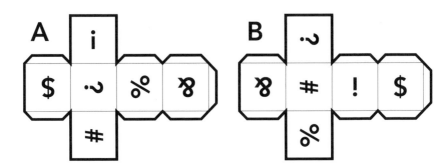

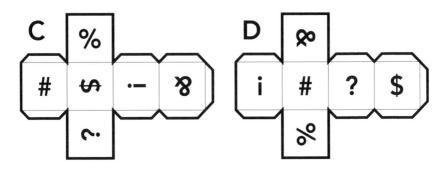

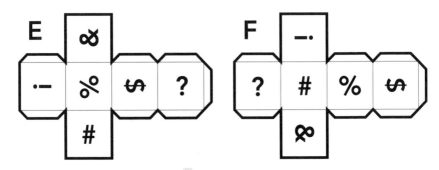

Black Holes 10

Divide the grid into chunks along the guides
provided so that each chunk contains one black
hole, and so the digits in the chunk sum to the
number in the black hole.

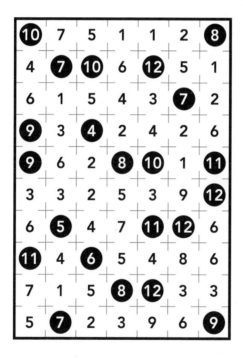

Symbol Sums 9

The sums of five combinations of symbols have been
provided. What is the value of each individual symbol?

🪐 ☆ ☆ ◎ → 38

◎ 🛸 👽 👽 → 39

🛸 👽 🪐 🪐 → 19

🪐 ◎ ☆ 🪐 → 30

🛸 🛸 👽 👽 → 30

☆	🪐	◎	🛸	👽

Tetra Grid 9

Drop each of the shapes into the grid in the order provided to spell ten six-letter words. Clues for the words have been provided next to the grid.

Actor's material

Golf location

Small, quick dinosaur

Convent occupant

Jewelry with storage

Live broadcast

Earned prize

A rainbow color

Format

Air pocket

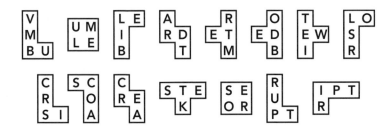

Numcross 9

Use the provided clues to fill the grid with numbers.
No entry may start with a 0.

A	B			C	D
E		F		G	
		H	I		
	J				
K			L	M	N
O				P	

Across

A.   A perfect square

C.   D down × 2

E.   A down × 3

G.   Another perfect square

H.   L across + N down

J.   P across × 4

K.   Another perfect square

L.   Another perfect square

O.   3 × K across

P.   K down + 4

Down

A.   C across – N down

B.   Digits that sum to N down

C.   A multiple of G across

D.   A across – M down

F.   C across × 6

I.   N down × P across

J.   P across × 5

K.   A perfect cube

M.   A across – D down

N.   Square root of L across

Chess Sudoku 5

Place a digit from 1 to 8 into each empty cell so that each row, column, and 3x3 block contains each digit once, without repetition. The chess knights in the grid display the sum of the digits in the cells which they can attack.

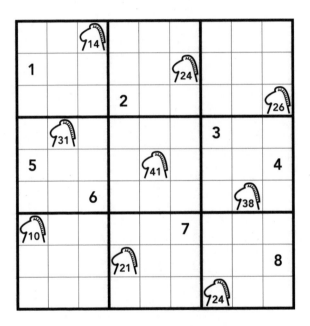

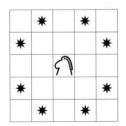

Tetra Grid 10A

Drop each of the shapes into the grid in the order
provided to spell ten different six-letter words. In
lieu of clues, these words form partial recipes.

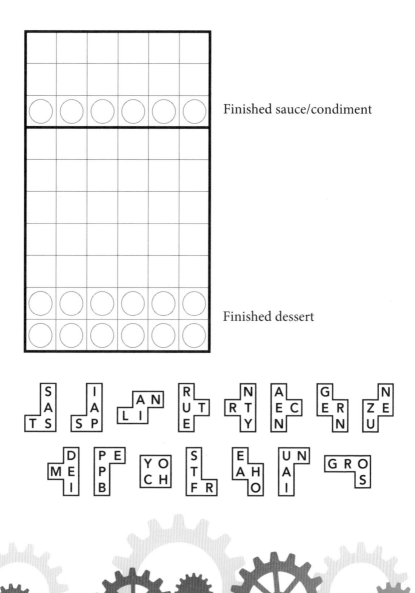

Finished sauce/condiment

Finished dessert

Tetra Grid 10B

Drop each of the shapes into the grid in the order
provided to spell ten different six-letter words. In
lieu of clues, these words form a partial recipe.

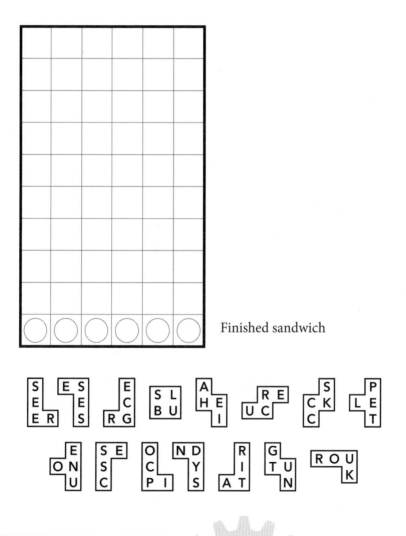

Finished sandwich

Numcross 10

Use the provided clues to fill the grid with numbers.
No entry may start with a 0.

A B			C D E			F G H		
I			J			K		
L	M				N			
	O		P Q					
R S			T			U V W		
X			Y			Z		
		AA			BB			
CC DD EE					FF		GG HH	
II			JJ KK			LL		
MM			NN			OO		

Across

A. A perfect square

C. A down – D down

F. Consecutive digits in ascending order

I. 2 × D down

J. B down in reverse

K. 2 × T across

L. An anagram of C down

N. GG down × I across

O. 12 × N across

R. CC down + 1

T. 5 × JJ down

U. GG down – 1

X. GG down – 5

Y. A perfect cube

Z. C across – N down

AA. Contains one of each odd digit

CC. 2 × G down

FF. B down × 12

II. Consecutive digits in ascending order

JJ. Another perfect square

LL. Another perfect square

MM. A palindrome

NN. G down + T across

OO. 2 × I across

Down

A. LL across × 4

B. J across in reverse

C. Z across × R down

D. R down - 1

E. Y across in reverse

F. X across × 4

G. Another palindrome

H. N down squared

M. One-fifth of AA across

N. D down + I across

P. The 'Summer of Love'

Q. Consecutive digits in descending order

R. D down + 1

S. Another perfect cube

U. 2 × MM across

V. R down × 8

W. Sum of the digits in the fifth column from left (D down, P down, and JJ down)

AA. Another perfect square

BB. M down in reverse

CC. I across + J across

DD. U across × 4

EE. H down + E down

GG. E down × 4

HH. N down × 7

JJ. KK down – N down

KK. Another perfect square

Black Holes 11

Divide the grid into chunks along the guides
provided so that each chunk contains one black
hole, and so the digits in the chunk sum to the
number in the black hole.

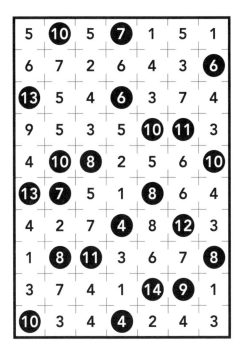

In Memoriam 4A

Memorize the images displayed below. When you're ready, turn the page and put your memory to the test.

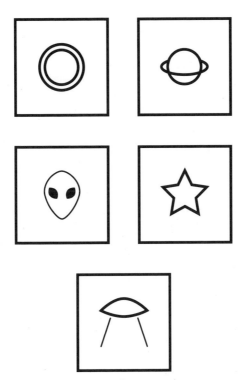

In Memoriam 4B

Moving up, down, left, and right, make a path from
Start to Finish. You may only pass through squares
containing an image displayed on the previous page.

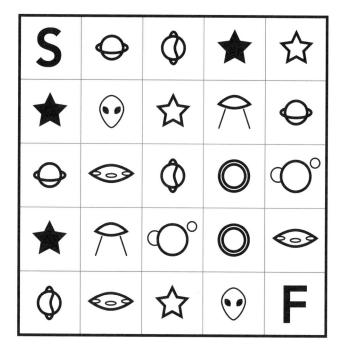

Chess Sudoku 6

Place a digit from 1 to 8 into each empty cell so that each row, column, and 3x3 block contains each digit once, without repetition. The chess knights in the grid display the sum of the digits in the cells which they can attack.

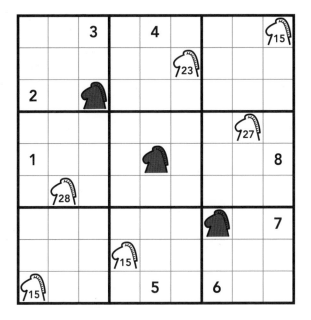

Tetra Grid 11

Drop each of the shapes into the grid in the order provided to spell ten six-letter words. Clues for the words have been provided next to the grid.

One in charge

Take away

Investments

Shower nuisance

Frugal person's clipping

Audible warnings

Type of card

Flowery quality

Potential sale location

Hot dog topper

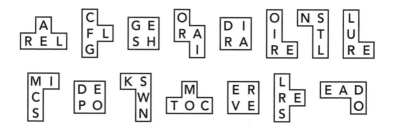

In Memoriam 5A

Memorize the numbers shown in the grid below.
When you're ready, turn the page and put your
memory to the test.

S	1	4	0	8
9	0	2	1	0
8	6	7	5	3
0	9	3	2	1
1	8	0	0	F

In Memoriam 5B

Moving up, down, left, and right, make a path from
Start to Finish. You may only pass through squares
where the number has not changed from the number
that was in the same square on the previous page.

S	1	4	0	8
7	1	1	9	0
8	6	7	5	3
4	0	4	2	6
1	8	8	0	F

Rearrangement 17–18

Rearrange the letters in the phrase "WORST ORACLE" to spell something useful for a painter pretending to be a psychic.

Rearrange the letters in the phrase "A TEST PHOTO" to spell a product often advertised with before and after photos.

Cube Logic 9

Which two of the six foldable patterns can be folded
to make the same cube?

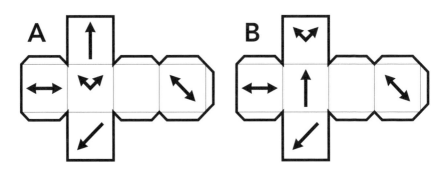

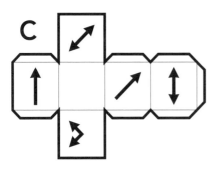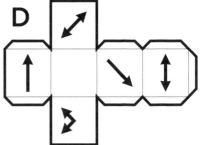

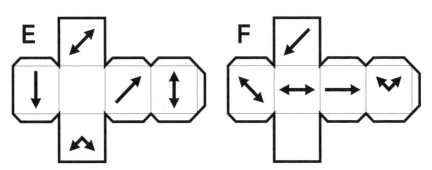

Rows Garden 8

Using the clues provided, enter a letter into each triangle to fill the garden. Each row contains one or two entries, and each hexagonal flower contains a six-letter word wrapped around the center. It's up to you to determine where to place the starting letter and the direction of the word.

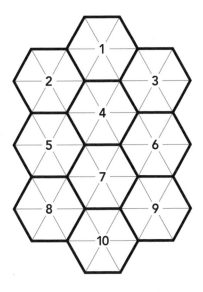

Primate

Inky sea-dweller/Judge

Rub out/Luxury hotel brand

Full range/Microsoft search engine

Disputed Asian region/Ugly giant

Oft-chaotic bird/Queue

Antagonists/"Double D" in toon trio

Common address suffix

Flowers

1. Made good on a loan
2. Simple shape
3. Convict
4. Absurd
5. Calculated risk
6. Spicy root
7. Mexican street corn
8. Legume nickname
9. Refused
10. Goes away

Tetra Grid 12A

Drop each of the shapes into the grid in the order provided to spell ten six-letter words. Clues for the words have been provided next to the grid.

X-Files agent

Root vegetable

Book creator

Ringed planet

Holey breakfast items

City in Minnesota

On the web?

Three-ringed noun

Secondary color

Health insurance add-on

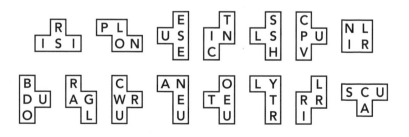

Tetra Grid 12B

Drop each of the shapes into the grid in the order provided to spell ten NEW six-letter words which match up with the clues from the previous puzzle.

X-Files agent

Root vegetable

Book creator

Ringed planet

Holey breakfast items

City in Minnesota

On the web?

Three-ringed noun

Secondary color

Health insurance add-on

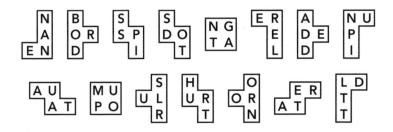

Numcross 11

Use the provided clues to fill the grid with numbers.
No entry may start with a 0.

A	B	C	D		E	F		G	H
I					J		K		
		L		M		N			
O	P		Q		R			S	T
U		V		W			X		
Y			Z				AA		
BB			CC			DD		EE	
		FF			GG		HH		
II	JJ			KK		LL		MM	NN
OO			PP			QQ			

Across

A. I across + 5000

E. E down – 1

G. One-fourth of S across

I. C down + 200

J. Consecutive digits in ascending order

L. B down × E across

N. NN down – 1

O. G across + 2

Q. Consecutive digits in descending order

S. EE across + 7

U. One-half of LL across

W. M down × KK down

Y. A palindrome

AA. EE across + MM down

BB. B down – 1

CC. An anagram of LL across

EE. LL across / S across

FF. A perfect cube

GG. KK down × X down

II. 2 × Z down

LL. Year that QQ across was released

OO. II down in reverse

PP. HH down – GG across

QQ. A Stanley Kubrick film

Down

A. G down in reverse

B. A down – K down

C. I across – 200

D. A down × B down × 5

E. B down × 3

F. C down × KK down

G. A perfect square

H. A perfect cube

K. MM down – BB across

M. Contains one of each even digit

O. LL across + 3

P. N across × MM down

R. Contains one of each odd digit

S. Another palindrome

T. Digits that sum to BB down

V. G down + KK down

X. KK down – 4

Z. One-half of II across

DD. G across × AA across

FF. FF across + 5

HH. GG across + PP across

II. Another perfect square

JJ. S across – KK down

KK. Another perfect square

MM. BB across × 6

NN. One more perfect square for good measure

Symbol Sums 10

The sums of five combinations of symbols have been
provided. What is the value of each individual symbol?

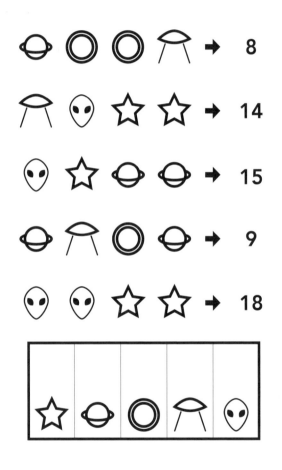

Rearrangement 19–20

Rearrange the letters in the phrase "INLAND PARLEY" to spell the place a pirate might write down a memo for such an event.

Rearrange the letters in the phrase "COOL TORMENTER" to spell something that could be used to interrupt a binge-watching session.

Black Holes 12

Divide the grid into chunks along the guides provided so that each chunk contains one black hole, and so the digits in the chunk sum to the number in the black hole.

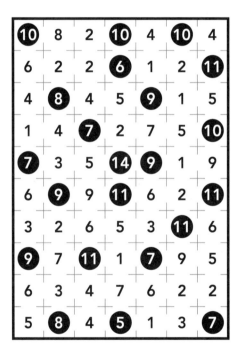

In Memoriam 6A

Memorize the numbers shown in the balls below.
When you're ready, turn the page and put your
memory to the test.

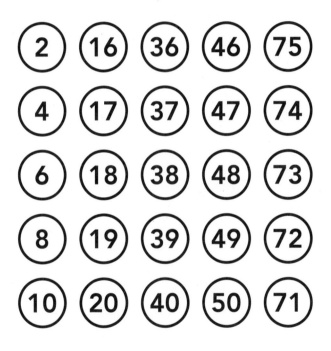

In Memoriam 6B

In the grid below, find the single row, column,
or diagonal that contains only numbers from the
previous page. (Yelling "BINGO" when you're done
is optional.)

2	29	32	56	75
6	17	39	46	72
8	28	Free Space	51	68
4	26	35	49	71
1	20	40	60	70

Tetra Grid 13

Drop each of the shapes into the grid in the order provided to spell ten six-letter words. Clues for the words have been provided next to the grid.

Sewing unit

Arrow holder

Type of mushroom

Leave

Smashing Pumpkins frontman

Pulse

Bed necessity

Heat

Workout component

Repaired

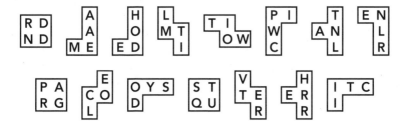

Cube Logic 10

Which two of the six foldable patterns can be folded
to make the same cube?

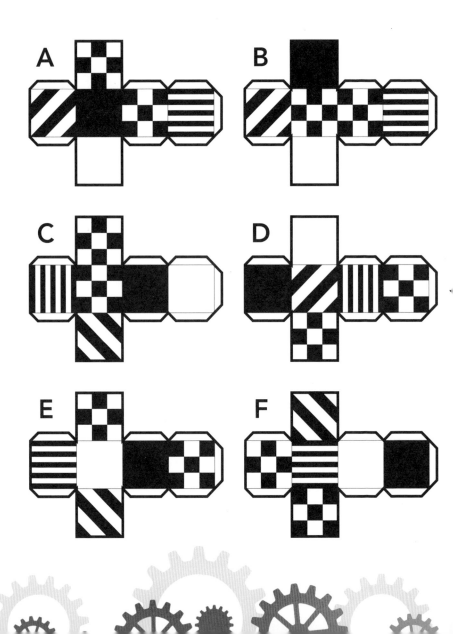

ANSWER KEYS

Black Holes 1

10	1	4	**4**	4	2	3
9	5	**9**	6	**9**	**9**	4
2	**11**	3	3	2	1	**6**
6	**8**	5	**6**	1	5	3
1	3	3	3	**11**	**10**	3
11	5	**12**	3	3	3	7
2	5	9	5	**6**	1	2
7	**9**	**10**	4	2	3	**9**
1	1	5	4	**8**	4	6
5	4	3	**7**	6	2	**9**

Black Holes 2

5	3	**8**	2	**6**	2	4
4	**11**	3	4	**13**	**6**	2
8	7	**9**	4	3	3	**7**
3	2	6	**4**	7	4	5
5	**6**	1	3	**10**	6	1
9	6	5	1	1	**11**	2
4	5	**11**	6	**7**	5	**9**
6	2	**8**	3	6	1	6
7	8	4	4	**9**	4	**6**
3	4	**12**	**6**	2	5	1

Black Holes 3

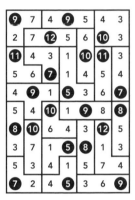

9	7	4	**9**	5	4	3
2	7	**12**	5	6	**10**	3
11	4	3	1	**10**	**11**	3
5	6	**7**	1	4	5	4
4	**9**	1	**5**	3	6	**7**
5	4	**10**	1	**9**	8	**8**
8	**10**	6	4	3	**12**	5
3	7	1	**5**	**8**	1	3
5	3	4	1	5	7	4
7	2	4	**5**	3	6	**9**

Black Holes 4

6	**9**	3	5	**6**	1	**9**
5	**6**	2	4	1	7	8
2	2	**10**	3	**12**	5	**11**
7	2	5	**13**	3	6	7
6	**8**	4	8	5	**9**	4
3	**9**	4	**12**	1	1	**6**
1	5	**8**	7	5	2	3
6	5	**11**	2	**5**	2	**8**
5	1	5	4	3	5	5
2	**7**	6	**5**	1	3	**8**

Black Holes 5

2	5	**6**	1	6	**5**	6
7	4	3	4	**7**	3	1
6	5	3	**7**	5	2	**7**
3	**9**	6	3	1	**6**	3
10	1	**10**	1	**5**	4	4
7	**8**	4	4	3	1	**8**
1	3	5	**7**	6	5	2
6	2	3	3	2	6	**7**
3	**10**	2	**4**	**14**	4	3
3	**10**	5	1	2	**10**	1

Black Holes 6

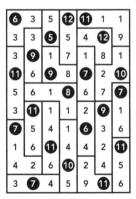

6	3	5	**12**	**11**	1	1
3	3	**5**	5	4	**12**	9
3	**9**	1	7	1	8	1
11	6	**9**	8	**7**	2	**10**
5	6	1	**8**	6	7	**7**
3	**11**	1	1	2	**9**	1
7	5	4	1	**6**	3	6
1	6	**11**	4	4	2	**11**
4	2	6	**10**	2	4	5
3	**7**	4	5	9	**11**	6

Black Holes 7

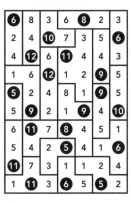

Black Holes 8

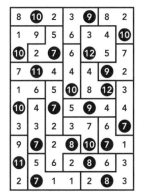

Black Holes 9

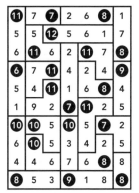

Black Holes 10

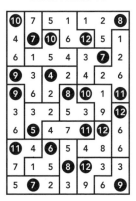

Black Holes 11

Black Holes 12

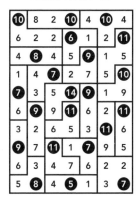

Chess Sudoku 1

4	5	2	7	3	6	8	♞	1
♞	1	6	8	2	4	5	3	7
8	7	3	1	5	♞	4	2	6
5	2	♞	3	8	7	1	6	4
6	4	7	2	♞	1	3	5	8
3	8	1	4	6	5	♞	7	2
7	3	8	♞	4	2	6	1	5
1	6	4	5	7	3	2	8	♞
2	♞	5	6	1	8	7	4	3

Chess Sudoku 2

1	7	8	6	4	♞	2	5	3
5	2	♞	3	7	1	8	6	4
4	6	3	5	2	8	1	♞	7
♞	5	7	4	8	2	3	1	6
3	1	2	7	♞	6	4	8	5
6	8	4	1	3	5	7	2	♞
7	♞	5	8	1	3	6	4	2
8	3	6	2	5	4	♞	7	1
2	4	1	♞	6	7	5	3	8

Chess Sudoku 3

7	6	1	3	4	8	♞	2	5
5	8	3	♞	7	2	1	6	4
♞	2	4	5	6	1	7	8	3
8	4	7	1	2	5	3	♞	5
2	1	5	6	♞	3	4	7	8
3	♞	6	4	8	7	2	5	1
6	7	2	8	1	4	5	3	♞
4	5	8	7	3	♞	6	1	2
1	3	♞	2	5	6	8	4	7

Chess Sudoku 4

5	7	1	6	4	8	♞	3	2
3	6	2	♞	1	7	5	4	8
♞	8	4	2	5	3	1	7	6
4	♞	7	3	8	2	6	5	1
6	1	8	4	♞	5	3	2	7
2	5	3	7	6	1	8	♞	4
7	2	5	8	3	6	4	1	♞
1	4	6	5	7	♞	2	8	3
8	3	♞	1	2	4	7	6	5

Chess Sudoku 5

2	8	♞	3	1	4	6	7	5
1	4	7	6	5	♞	8	2	3
3	6	5	2	7	8	4	1	♞
4	♞	2	1	8	5	3	6	7
5	1	3	7	♞	6	2	8	4
8	7	6	4	2	3	5	♞	1
♞	3	4	8	6	7	1	5	2
6	5	1	♞	4	2	7	3	8
7	2	8	5	3	1	♞	4	6

Chess Sudoku 6

8	5	3	6	4	7	2	1	♞
6	7	1	5	2	♞	8	3	4
2	4	♞	1	8	3	5	7	6
4	6	8	3	7	5	1	♞	2
1	3	5	2	♞	4	7	6	8
7	♞	2	8	1	6	3	4	5
5	8	6	4	3	1	♞	2	7
3	2	7	♞	6	8	4	5	1
♞	1	4	7	5	2	6	8	3

Cube Logic

1:	Pattern D	6:	Pattern D
2:	Pattern A	7:	Pattern B
3:	Pattern C	8:	Patterns B and F
4:	Pattern B	9:	Patterns A and C
5:	Pattern A	10:	Patterns D and F

In Memoriam 1

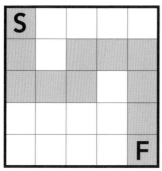

In Memoriam 2

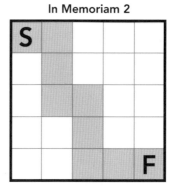

In Memoriam 3

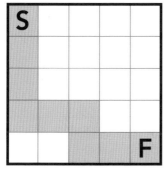

In Memoriam 4

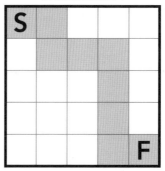

In Memoriam 5

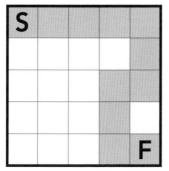

In Memoriam 6

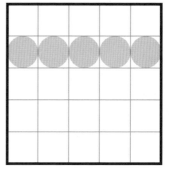

Numcross 1

Numcross 2

Numcross 3

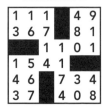

Numcross 4

Numcross 5

Numcross 6

Numcross 7

Numcross 8

Numcross 9

Numcross 10

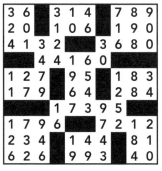

Numcross 11

Rearrangement

1:	Coffee Filters	11:	Radio Station
2:	Batman and Robin	12:	Cell Signal
3:	Railroad Crossing	13:	Cast-Iron Pan
4:	Thirty Yard Line	14:	Commuter Train
5:	Roller Coasters	15:	Space Shuttle
6:	Texas Panhandle	16:	Fitted Sheets
7:	Ariana Grande	17:	Watercolors
8:	Chinese Takeout	18:	Toothpaste
9:	Binge Watching	19:	Daily Planner
10:	Income Taxes	20:	Remote Control

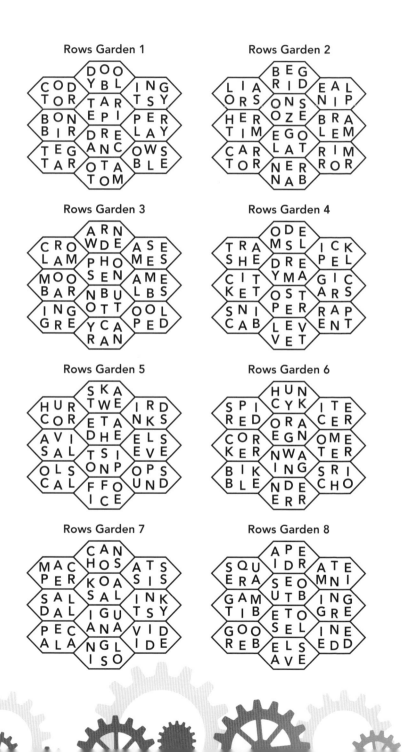

Story Logic 1   Section 1: a cavern, with Mekala dressed as a skeleton
Section 2: a crypt, with Kiera dressed as a vampire
Section 3: a jail, with Jared dressed as a zombie
Section 4: a cemetery, with Nupur dressed as a goblin
Section 5: a sawmill, with Landon dressed as a mummy

Story Logic 2   Sunday's class at Georgie's is a sugar skull painting
Monday's class at The Brewery is a winter scene painting
Tuesday's class at Tres Amigas is a painting of mountains
Wednesday's class at The Tin Panther is a sunset painting

Story Logic 3   At 2.5 mi., a 60 ft. bridge dedicated to Becky Lynch
At 2.7 mi., a 20 ft. bridge dedicated to Leah Remini
At 8.1 mi., a 40 ft. bridge dedicated to Guy Fieri
At 8.3 mi., a 32 ft. bridge dedicated to Adam Savage
At 9.0 mi., a 48 ft. bridge dedicated to David Biedny

Story Logic 4   In 5th place, Amy's Cheezy Cauliflower Queso Dip
In 4th place, Carol's Smoked Almond Cheeze Ball
In 3rd place, Dirk's Nooch-oh Cheeze Sauce
In 2nd place, Eileen's Carrot Cheddar Chunks
In 1st place, Breighdynn's Wild Garlic Walnut Gouda Spread

Symbol Sums 1

5	8	4	11	7
☆	♁	◎	⊓	👽

Symbol Sums 2

25	7	17	8	1
☆	♁	◎	⊓	👽

Symbol Sums 3

2	5	6	8	11
☆	♁	◎	⊓	👽

Symbol Sums 4

16	12	8	4	24
☆	♁	◎	⊓	👽

Symbol Sums 5

11	5	2	8	19
☆	♁	◎	⊓	👽

Symbol Sums 6

21	13	3	8	9
☆	♁	◎	⊓	👽

Symbol Sums 7

10	15	4	14	2
☆	♁	◎	⊓	👽

Symbol Sums 8

6	8	15	32	11
☆	♁	◎	⊓	👽

Symbol Sums 9

10	2	16	7	8
☆	♁	◎	⊓	👽

Symbol Sums 10

4	3	2	1	5
☆	♁	◎	⊓	👽

Tetra Grid 1

```
C O P P E R
C H A T T Y
F R I D G E
S E L D O M
C I T R U S
F I L T E R
P O C K E T
S T R E E T
E N I G M A
M O N D A Y
```

Tetra Grid 2

```
A N I M A L
T O M A T O
P E A N U T
L U M B E R
B A T T L E
F I E S T A
H E A R T S
E L E V E N
B R I G H T
S C R U B S
```

Tetra Grid 3

```
S P R I N G
W A S H E R
T R I V I A
K E R N E L
S P R O U T
B R U N C H
F R I G I D
D E X T E R
P O L A N D
G R A I N Y
```

Tetra Grid 4

```
F A U C E T
K I D N E Y
S M O O T H
C I R C L E
H O L L O W
B U T T E R
S I M P L E
D A N I S H
T R A V E L
S T A M P S
```

Tetra Grid 5

```
L E A V E S
S H R I M P
M A S C O T
D R I V E N
L I Q U O R
T A T T O O
M A T U R E
V E N D O R
B R I D G E
G R A V E L
```

Tetra Grid 6

```
E R A S E R
R E T U R N
L I C H E N
O R E G O N
W A F F L E
M E T E R S
R E V I V E
D E C A D E
C A N D L E
T R A G I C
```

Tetra Grid 7

```
E N E R G Y
A L M O S T
S P I C E D
L I Q U I D
A S S U M E
U R G E N T
S M O K E R
M I N I O N
B A R B E R
U N R E A D
```

Tetra Grid 8

```
D R I V E R
Y A N K E E
C O U G A R
S I Z Z L E
M A R K E R
S E N A T E
A M B U S H
C A M E R A
V O W E L S
P O L I C Y
```

Tetra Grid 9

```
S C R I P T
C O U R S E
R A P T O R
S I S T E R
L O C K E T
S T R E A M
R E W A R D
V I O L E T
M E D I U M
B U B B L E
```

Tetra Grid 10A

```
G R O U N D
S E S A M E
T A H I N I
F R O Z E N
Y O G U R T
C H E R R Y
P E A N U T
P I E C E S
B A N A N A
S P L I T S
```

Tetra Grid 10B

```
G R O U N D
T U R K E Y
O N I O N S
C A T S U P
P I C K L E
S E C R E T
S A U C E S
C H E E S E
S L I C E S
B U R G E R
```

Tetra Grid 11

```
L E A D E R
R E M O V E
S T O C K S
M I L D E W
C O U P O N
S I R E N S
C R E D I T
F L O R A L
G A R A G E
R E L I S H
```

Tetra Grid 12A

```
S C U L L Y
C A R R O T
W R I T E R
U R A N U S
B A G E L S
D U L U T H
O N L I N E
C I R C U S
P U R P L E
V I S I O N
```

Tetra Grid 12B

```
M U L D E R
P O T A T O
A U T H O R
S A T U R N
D O N U T S
S T P A U L
S P I D E R
B I N D E R
O R A N G E
D E N T A L
```

Tetra Grid 13

```
S T I T C H
Q U I V E R
O Y S T E R
D E P A R T
C O R G A N
L E N T I L
P I L L O W
W A R M T H
C A R D I O
M E N D E D
```

Exercise Your Mind at American Mensa

At American Mensa, we love puzzles. In fact, we have events—large and small—centered around games and puzzles.

Of course, at 55,000 members and growing, we're much more than that, with members aged 2 to 102 and from all walks of life. Our one shared trait might be one you share too: high intelligence, measured in the top 2 percent of the general public in a standardized test.

Get-togethers with other Mensans—from small pizza nights up to larger events like our annual Mind Games—are always stimulating and fun. Roughly 130 Special Interest Groups (we call them SIGs) offer the best of the real and virtual worlds. Highlighting the Mensa newsstand is our award-winning magazine, *Mensa Bulletin*, which stimulates the curious mind with unique features that add perspective to our fast-paced world.

And then there are the practical benefits of membership, such as exclusive offers through our partners and member discounts on magazine subscriptions, online shopping, and financial services.

Find out how to qualify or take our practice test at americanmensa.org/join.